English for IT Professionals

A COMPLETE GUIDE TO IMPROVE YOUR TECHNICAL ENGLISH SKILLS IN THE IT FIELD

Introduction

Chapter 1: Welcome to Technical English!

Chapter 2: Learning Tech Words and Making Them Stick

Chapter 3: Getting Comfortable with IT Concepts and Processes

Chapter 4: Reading Comprehension in Technical Contexts

Chapter 5: Verbal Communication in IT

Chapter 6: Technical English in Different IT Domains

Chapter 7: Common Mistakes in Technical English

Chapter 8: Enhancing Technical English Skills

Conclusion: Resource Bank

Introduction

Imagine a career where your technical expertise isn't just impressive—it's unstoppable. Where your ability to communicate with precision and clarity breaks barriers, unlocks opportunities, and sets you apart as a true global IT leader. In the tech world, where innovation knows no borders, mastering English is no longer optional—it's the key to thriving in an industry that runs on collaboration, creativity, and cutting-edge solutions.

English for IT Professionals is your ultimate guide to mastering the language that powers the tech world. This book goes beyond grammar and vocabulary—it's a transformative toolkit for professionals who aspire to lead, connect, and excel in a global IT environment.

Inside, you'll discover:

- **Tech-Specific Vocabulary and Skills**: Speak the language of coding, troubleshooting, and innovation with fluency and confidence.
- **Real-World Scenarios and Case Studies:** Step into the shoes of IT experts handling high-stakes challenges, and learn how to communicate solutions like a pro.

- **Advanced Communication Strategies:** Write emails that resonate, lead meetings that inspire, and craft documentation that's clear and effective.
- **Continuous Learning Resources:** Access a curated list of cutting-edge tools, platforms, and communities to keep your language and tech skills sharp.

This isn't just a language book—it's your passport to global success in IT. Whether you're a budding programmer or a seasoned professional, this guide equips you with the linguistic confidence to tackle technical challenges, communicate seamlessly with international teams, and make your mark in the fast-evolving tech industry.

English for IT Professionals is more than a book—it's a career-changing opportunity. With every chapter, you'll sharpen your English, unlock new dimensions of your potential, and take one step closer to becoming a world-class IT professional.

Get ready to level up your language, supercharge your career, and join the ranks of IT professionals who lead, innovate, and inspire across the globe.

Let's build the future—one word, one line of code, and one breakthrough at a time. Welcome to your next big step in IT mastery!

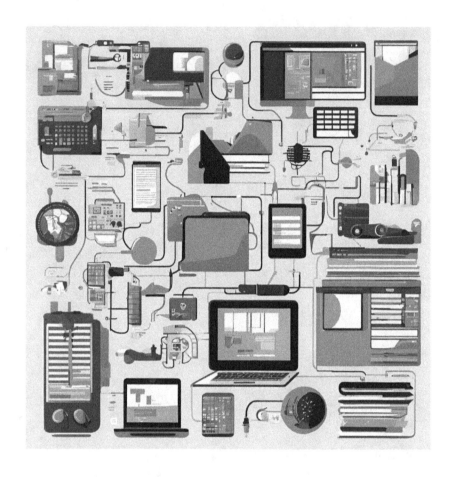

Chapter One
Welcome to Technical English

Why IT Folks Need Technical English

Okay, picture this: You're working on an exciting tech project with a super cool team. Your team members come from different countries and speak different languages. One person is a software developer, another is a project manager, and there's even a client who doesn't really know much about tech. How do you explain your brilliant ideas and get everyone on the same page? The magic word here is *Technical English*!

Technical English is like a special language that helps IT professionals talk about tricky tech stuff without confusing anyone. Whether it's writing a report, having a meeting, or collaborating on a project, being able to speak and understand Technical English is your secret weapon.

Here's why it's so important:

- **Working Across Borders**: IT is a global industry. Whether you're working with someone in the next office or halfway around the world, having a common language means you can all understand each other, even if you speak different native languages.
- **Sharing Ideas Clearly**: It's not just about knowing English—it's about knowing the *right* words for the job. Instead of saying "that's complicated," you can use specific words like "API," "machine learning," or

"cloud computing" to describe exactly what you mean.

- **Being Part of the Global Conversation**: The tech world is constantly changing. And guess what? Most of the updates, research, and resources come in English. If you're fluent in Technical English, you can join the global tech conversations, learn the latest trends, and stay ahead of the curve.

So, whether you're chatting with a colleague in another country, reading the newest tech article, or giving a presentation, Technical English helps you do it better, faster, and more confidently.

Why It's the Tech World's "Universal Language"

IT is huge—like, global huge. Tech companies are everywhere, and they all need a way to communicate. That's where Technical English comes in. It's the "universal language" that everyone in the tech world uses to get stuff done. If you want to be part of this fast-moving, ever-changing world, you need to speak the language!

Here's why learning Technical English is a game-changer:

- **International Projects**: The best tech projects often have teams from all over the world. Imagine collaborating with someone from Brazil, another person from India, and a client in the U.S. How do you all talk? Simple! You use Technical English. It's the go-to language for global tech collaboration.

- **Learning from the Best**: Want to learn about the latest programming language? Or maybe there's a new way to protect your data from hackers? Most of the best resources—like books, blogs, tutorials, and research papers—are written in English. If you can read and understand Technical English, you get access to all that awesome knowledge.
- **Shining in Your Career**: The more you master Technical English, the better you can present your ideas, write reports, and impress your boss. When you can explain your work clearly and confidently, people will start noticing. And that could mean promotions, new opportunities, or even getting to work on the most exciting projects!

Let's Talk Tech Words

Every job has its own lingo, right? Like, if you're a gamer, you probably use words like "XP," "loot," and "level up." In IT, we have our own special language. These words and phrases are *essential* if you want to understand what's going on in the tech world.

You've probably heard some of these terms before, like:

- **Cloud Computing**: The internet! But it's more than just browsing websites—it's about storing data and running applications online instead of on your computer.

- **API (Application Programming Interface)**: A way for different software programs to talk to each other. It's like a waiter taking your order and delivering it to the kitchen in a restaurant.
- **Machine Learning**: Computers that can learn and improve without being told exactly what to do, just like how humans learn from experience.

These are just a few of the *many* words you'll come across in IT. But it's not just about knowing these terms—it's about understanding them deeply. Once you get familiar with tech jargon, you'll feel more confident when talking about your work and collaborating with others.

And guess what? Every part of IT has its own special vocabulary. For example:

- Cybersecurity pros know terms like "malware," "firewall," and "encryption."
- Developers use words like "algorithm," "repository," and "debugging."

The more words you know, the easier it is to share your thoughts, ask questions, and solve problems. And with new tech coming out all the time, there's always something new to learn!

Common Challenges: Don't Worry, You Got This!

Okay, let's be real: Technical English can be tricky at first. But don't stress! Everyone goes through it, and with some practice, you'll get better every day. Here are a few challenges you might face—and how to crush them:

1. **Tech Talk Overload**: IT can feel like a language of its own, full of acronyms and confusing terms. Don't worry if you don't understand everything at first! Break it down, ask questions, and soon you'll be talking like a pro.
2. **Different Levels of Knowledge**: Sometimes, you'll talk to people who know a lot about tech—and sometimes, you'll talk to people who know very little. This can make it tricky to explain things. But here's the trick: Be patient, simplify your words, and use analogies. You can explain complex ideas in easy ways!
3. **Time Pressure**: IT moves fast. You may have deadlines to meet, and sometimes that means rushing to finish reports or projects. But don't skip the details! Good communication takes time. When you're writing or presenting, make sure your message is clear and well-organized.
4. **Cultural Differences**: You'll likely work with people from all over the world, and different cultures have different ways of communicating. Some cultures like a lot of details, while others prefer things to be

direct. Being aware of these differences will help you avoid misunderstandings.

5. **Tools and Visuals**: Diagrams, charts, and screenshots can be super helpful—but they can also confuse people if they're not clear. Make sure your visuals are easy to read, labeled correctly, and show exactly what you mean. Also, make sure your digital tools (like video calls or presentations) are working smoothly!

By practicing your Technical English and staying aware of these challenges, you'll keep improving your communication skills. You'll be able to explain your ideas clearly, work with people from all over the world, and build your career.

Conclusion: The Future is Yours!

Mastering Technical English isn't just about learning new words—it's about opening doors to new opportunities. You'll be able to communicate clearly, collaborate with a global team, stay updated with the latest tech trends, and make a bigger impact in your career. Plus, you'll feel more confident when talking about your work and sharing your ideas with others.

So, let's get started! The world of tech is waiting, and with your Technical English skills, you're ready to conquer it!

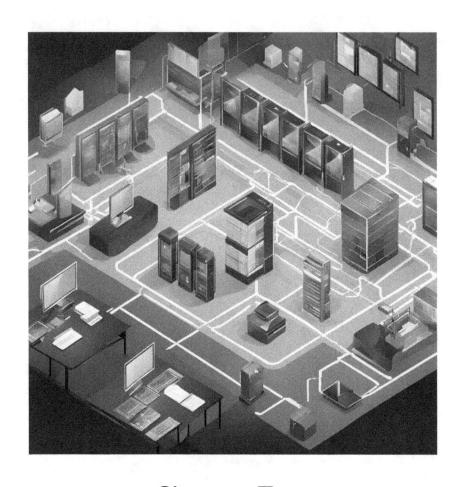

Chapter Two
Learning Tech Words and Making Them Stick

Must-Know IT Words

To be an IT pro, you need to know some key words. These words are like the building blocks that help you understand and talk about all the cool (and sometimes complicated!) stuff going on in the tech world. In this chapter, we'll break down some of the most important IT terms that you'll come across every day. Don't worry if you're new to these—once you learn them, you'll feel much more comfortable using them when you work with others!

Let's dive into some key terms that you should get familiar with:

Cloud Computing

Cloud computing is everywhere. Imagine having all your files, apps, and data stored somewhere far away, but you can access them anytime, anywhere, as long as you have an internet connection. That's the cloud! It's like using a virtual hard drive on the internet instead of keeping everything on your computer.

For example, when you use **Google Drive** to store your photos or files, you're using cloud computing. You can access them from any device, as long as you log into your Google account.

Cloud computing has different types of services:

- **IaaS (Infrastructure as a Service)**: This is like renting computers in the cloud. Companies don't need to own all the physical servers. Instead, they rent server space and computing power as they need it. For example, Amazon Web Services (AWS) offers IaaS, letting businesses rent virtual servers to run their websites.
- **PaaS (Platform as a Service)**: This gives developers tools and services to build applications, without worrying about the infrastructure behind them. Think of **Google App Engine**: it lets developers build apps without needing to manage the servers themselves.
- **SaaS (Software as a Service)**: This is software that you use online, like **Netflix**, **Spotify**, or **Dropbox**. These apps are hosted in the cloud, so you don't need to install anything or worry about updates. You just log in and start using them!

Virtualization

Virtualization is the tech magic that allows you to run multiple operating systems or programs on a single computer. Imagine you have one super-powerful computer, but instead of just using it for one job, you divide it into different parts. Each part runs its own system! This helps save money, space, and time.

A good example is **virtual machines**. Let's say you need to test a new app, but you don't want to risk messing up your computer. Using virtualization, you can create a "fake" computer inside your real computer. You can install the app on this fake computer and test it out safely, without affecting your actual system.

For instance, a company might use **VMware** or **Microsoft Hyper-V** to create multiple virtual machines on a single server, each running different tasks like hosting a website or running a database.

Big Data

Big Data is all about collecting and analyzing large amounts of information. Think about all the data created by websites, apps, and devices every day: your social media posts, your emails, and your online shopping. That's big data!

For example, **Netflix** uses big data to recommend movies and shows. It looks at the huge amount of data on what you've watched before, what others like you are watching, and even the time of day you watch. This helps Netflix predict what you might enjoy next. The same idea applies to **Amazon**, which uses big data to suggest products based on your past purchases and browsing history.

Big data is powerful because it can help businesses make better decisions. But to understand and use it, professionals need special tools to sort through all the data. Terms like **data mining** (the process of discovering patterns) and **data lakes** (huge pools of raw data) are key to working with big data.

Cybersecurity

In today's digital world, protecting your data is more important than ever, and that's where cybersecurity comes in. Cybersecurity is all about keeping your computer systems and information safe from bad actors like hackers. It's like building a digital lock to protect your data from being stolen.

For example, when you use **two-factor authentication (2FA)** on your email or bank account, you're adding an extra layer of security. First, you enter your password (the first factor), then you get a text or app notification with a code (the second factor) that you must enter before you can access your account.

Cybersecurity also involves protecting against viruses, malware (malicious software), and even physical security—making sure that only authorized people can access a company's computers.

The Power of Acronyms

In the IT world, acronyms are everywhere! They're like shortcuts that save you time and help you talk faster. Once you learn the most common ones, you'll feel like a tech expert in no time. Here are some important ones to know:

Basic Acronyms

- **IT**: This stands for **Information Technology**. It's the umbrella term for everything related to computers and technology. This includes hardware (physical tech), software (programs), and networking (how things connect).
- **API: Application Programming Interface**. Think of it like a menu at a restaurant. When you order food, the waiter brings your order to the kitchen. Similarly, when you use an API, you're telling one software to do something for you by using a predefined "menu" of instructions.
- **VPN: Virtual Private Network**. It's like creating a secret tunnel on the internet so no one can see your online activity. For example, when you use a public Wi-Fi at a coffee shop, a VPN ensures your data stays private and secure.

Cybersecurity Acronyms

- **DDoS: Distributed Denial of Service**. This is a type of attack where hackers flood a website with too much traffic, making it crash. For example, a website like **Twitter** might go down if it's hit with a DDoS attack.

- **MFA: Multi-Factor Authentication**. This is a security measure that requires you to provide more than one way to prove your identity. Think about how you might need both a password and a code sent to your phone to log into your online banking account.

Software Development Acronyms

- **CI/CD: Continuous Integration/Continuous Deployment**. This is the practice of constantly updating and testing software. It's like making small changes to your code every day and checking to make sure it's still working properly before making it available to users.
- **OOP: Object-Oriented Programming**. This is a way to organize code by treating everything as an "object." Each object has data and functions that describe what it does. For example, an "object" might be a "car," with properties like "color" and "engine type," and methods like "drive" or "stop."

Tips for Learning New Tech Words

Now that you know some key terms and acronyms, how do you make sure you remember them? The good news is, there are lots of fun ways to keep expanding your vocabulary and making sure these tech words stick! Let's dive into a few easy strategies:

1. Read Tech Stuff

The best way to get familiar with new words is by reading about them. Start with tech blogs, articles, or guides. You don't have to read super complex books—just find something interesting and start learning! Websites like **TechCrunch**, **Wired**, and **Medium** are great places to find articles on the latest tech trends.

When you read about topics like cloud computing, cybersecurity, or AI, you'll see the terms in context, helping you understand how they're used in real-life scenarios.

2. Join Online Tech Communities

There are tons of online places where tech pros talk about everything from coding to cloud services. Websites like **Stack Overflow**, **GitHub**, and **LinkedIn groups** are perfect for getting involved. By asking questions or reading answers, you'll come across new terms and see how other people use them. For example, you might join a **cloud computing forum** to discuss the pros and cons of IaaS vs. SaaS.

You can also follow hashtags on Twitter, like **#CloudComputing** or **#AI** to stay updated on industry conversations.

3. Use Flashcards

Need a fun way to remember terms? Try flashcards! Apps like **Quizlet** or **Anki** let you create flashcards with the new terms you're learning. For example, you can create a flashcard for **API** and write the definition on one side and an example on the other side. The apps use special algorithms to help you review terms regularly until they're stuck in your memory.

4. Go to Workshops

Many companies and organizations host training events or workshops where you can practice using tech words in real situations. These events give you the chance to learn from experts and get hands-on experience. For instance, a cloud computing workshop might teach you how to set up your first virtual machine, and you'll learn the words and phrases that come with it.

5. Write About It

A great way to remember what you learn is by writing about it. Try starting a blog, writing a post on LinkedIn, or even contributing to a tech forum. Explaining things in your own words helps reinforce the vocabulary. If you can explain **big data** or **virtualization** to someone else, you know you've got it down.

Wrap-Up: Keep Expanding Your Tech Vocabulary!

As an IT professional, knowing the right vocabulary can make you feel like a superhero in the tech world. The more you learn and use these key terms and acronyms, the easier it will be to collaborate, solve problems, and explain complex ideas.

And the best part? You're always learning new words! Technology moves fast, and with every new tool or breakthrough, there's always something exciting to discover. Keep reading, asking questions, and practicing, and you'll continue to expand your vocabulary, making you even more awesome in your career!

Chapter Three
Getting Comfortable with IT
Concepts and Processes

Mastering IT Concepts for Clear Communication

When you're diving into the world of IT, understanding key concepts is as important as knowing the technical jargon. In this chapter, we'll walk through some foundational ideas and processes in IT that are essential for professionals to get comfortable with. These concepts are like the building blocks of IT projects, and understanding them will help you communicate clearly, solve problems efficiently, and work with clients, teammates, and stakeholders without a hitch.

Let's break down some of the most important concepts that you'll encounter as an IT pro:

The Software Development Life Cycle (SDLC)

The **Software Development Life Cycle (SDLC)** is a structured approach to designing, developing, and maintaining software. It's like a roadmap for building software and ensuring it meets users' needs while staying on budget and on time. There are different models for SDLC, but they all follow a similar process:

1. **Planning**: This is where you figure out what the software needs to do. You gather all the requirements and create a roadmap for the project.

   Real-world example: Imagine a company wants to build an online shopping platform. In the planning phase, the team would gather input from the marketing department, customer support, and potential users to understand exactly what features the site needs—like product search, payment gateways, and user reviews.

2. **Design**: In this stage, you start outlining the software's architecture—basically, how the software will be structured. Think of it as creating blueprints for a building before you start building.

    Real-world example: For the online shopping platform, the design phase would involve the UI/UX team creating wireframes of how the website will look and how users will navigate through it. The backend team would design the database and server architecture to ensure everything runs smoothly.

3. **Development**: This is where the actual coding happens! Developers write the code based on the design specifications.

    Real-world example: The developers start writing the actual code for the website, working with programming languages like HTML, CSS, JavaScript, and backend technologies such as Node.js or Python.

4. **Testing**: Before the software goes live, it has to be thoroughly tested to make sure it works as expected. This includes checking for bugs, glitches, and any issues that could affect the user experience.

    Real-world example: The testing phase for the online shopping platform would involve manual and automated tests. Testers would check for things like broken links, slow page load times, and errors during the checkout process.

5. **Deployment**: Once testing is complete, the software is deployed (released) for users. It's like launching a new product!

    Real-world example: After all the bugs have been fixed and everything is working well, the platform goes live. Customers can now access the site, browse products, and make purchases.

6. **Maintenance**: After the software is live, it still needs to be monitored and updated regularly to fix bugs, add new features, and ensure everything is running smoothly.

    Real-world example: After launch, the team would monitor the platform for any issues, such as security vulnerabilities or performance bottlenecks. They may also add new features based on customer feedback, like a wish list feature or the ability to save payment methods.

Agile Methodology

You've probably heard the term **Agile** thrown around. Agile is a methodology used in software development (and many other industries) that focuses on delivering small, working pieces of software quickly, instead of waiting for one huge release. Agile emphasizes flexibility and collaboration, making it a popular choice in the fast-paced tech world.

In Agile, projects are broken down into smaller **sprints** (think of sprints as mini-projects within the bigger project). After each sprint, the team evaluates what's been done, adjusts the plan if needed, and moves forward. It's like getting closer and closer to the finish line with each small step, instead of trying to get everything done all at once.

Real-world example: Suppose a company is building a mobile app for fitness tracking. In an Agile environment, the team might have a two-week sprint where they focus on building just the user registration feature. Once that's completed, they'll review the work and move to the next sprint, which could involve integrating workout tracking features. This approach allows the company to release functional parts of the app to users quickly and gather feedback, instead of waiting months for a complete app.

DevOps: Bridging the Gap Between Development and Operations

DevOps is all about breaking down the walls between developers (who write the code) and operations teams (who maintain the servers and infrastructure). It's a culture and set of practices that encourages collaboration and automation to improve the speed and quality of software development.

Think of DevOps like this: instead of developers creating software and then throwing it over the fence to the operations team to handle, both groups work together throughout the entire process. From planning to coding to deployment, everyone is involved and continuously improving the system.

Real-world example: Let's say a company is working on an e-commerce platform, and the development team has just finished adding a new payment gateway. Thanks to the DevOps model, the code is automatically pushed through a **CI/CD pipeline** (Continuous Integration/Continuous Deployment) to be tested and deployed. The operations team is immediately involved, making sure the code works seamlessly with the infrastructure and that there are no performance issues.

Network Architecture and Topology

Network architecture is the design of a computer network. It outlines how different devices, servers, and systems are connected and how data flows between them. A well-designed network makes sure that your systems run smoothly, securely, and efficiently.

In network design, **topology** refers to how different devices (like computers, printers, and servers) are arranged and connected in a network. There are several common types of topologies:

Real-world examples:

1. **Bus topology**: Think of a small office with all employees connected via a single cable. If that cable fails, everyone loses connection. In a larger business, this would be problematic.
2. **Star topology**: This is the most common setup for home and office networks, where devices (like laptops, printers, and phones) are all connected to a central hub or router. If one device fails, the rest of the network stays up and running.
3. **Ring topology**: A company with an office in multiple countries may use a ring network where data is passed in a loop from one office to another. If one connection goes down, the data can still be rerouted.

4. **Mesh topology**: A large data center might use mesh topology, where every device is connected to every other device to ensure maximum redundancy and fault tolerance. This setup is costly but ensures that if one link fails, the data can still reach its destination through other paths.

Databases: The Backbone of Information

A **database** is a system that stores and organizes data, making it easy to access, manage, and update. Think of it as an organized digital filing cabinet where everything is sorted into neat categories.

There are two main types of databases:

- **Relational databases**: These databases organize data into tables with rows and columns (like a spreadsheet). The most popular relational database system is **SQL** (Structured Query Language), used to manage data in a relational database. For example, **MySQL** or **PostgreSQL**.

  Real-world example: A small e-commerce company might use MySQL to store customer orders, product information, and inventory data. The customer orders would be kept in one table, and each order's details (like items purchased and prices) would be stored in another related table.

- **NoSQL databases**: These are used for handling unstructured data that doesn't fit neatly into tables. They're used for things like big data applications, real-time data, and content management systems. Examples include **MongoDB** and **Cassandra**.

  Real-world example: A social media platform like Facebook uses NoSQL databases (e.g., Cassandra) to handle the massive amount of unstructured data it generates, such as posts, comments, images, and videos. These systems allow for fast and efficient processing of data across multiple servers.

IT Processes: Key Workflow Essentials

In addition to understanding IT concepts, it's also important to get familiar with the processes that make the magic happen. Here are a few core IT processes that you'll encounter:

Incident Management

Incident management is the process of handling unexpected problems in IT systems—like when a server goes down, or a user can't access a website. The goal of incident management is to restore normal service as quickly as possible.

Real-world example: Let's say an online retailer's website crashes due to high traffic. The incident managemnet team will quickly identify the cause (maybe a server overload), take steps to resolve it (add more server capacity), and keep users informed while the issue is fixed.

Change Management

In IT, change management refers to the process of planning, implementing, and monitoring changes to systems or software. The goal is to make sure that changes are made safely without introducing new problems.

Real-world example: Imagine a company needs to upgrade its internal payroll system to accommodate new tax regulations. Change management would involve assessing the impact of the change, testing the upgrade in a controlled environment, and then gradually rolling it out to ensure smooth implementation.

Problem Management

Problem management is closely related to incident management, but it focuses on identifying the root cause of recurring issues and fixing them long-term. While incident management is all about putting out the fire, problem management is about finding out why the fire started in the first place and preventing it from happening again.

Real-world example: If users keep experiencing slow login times on an application, the problem management team might trace the issue to a database query that's running inefficiently. They would optimize the query to resolve the issue permanently.

Wrap-Up: Becoming Fluent in IT Concepts

Understanding key IT concepts and processes is a must for any IT professional. It's not just about memorizing terms—it's about grasping how these concepts fit into the bigger picture and how they work together to keep tech systems running smoothly. Whether you're diving into the **SDLC**, learning about **Agile**, or exploring **network topology**, these concepts will help you navigate the world of IT with confidence.

The more you understand these processes and frameworks, the easier it will be to communicate effectively with your team, contribute to projects, and solve complex problems. As you gain more experience, you'll see how these concepts apply to real-world scenarios, and that will help you become even better at what you do.

Chapter Four
Reading Comprehension in
Technical Contexts

Understanding Technical Manuals and Guides

Technical manuals and guides are essential tools for IT professionals. These documents provide in-depth instructions on everything from setting up hardware and software to troubleshooting and maintenance. For IT professionals, the ability to navigate these manuals effectively can make all the difference when it comes to solving problems or optimizing systems.

A typical technical manual is structured in a way that makes it easier for users to find relevant information quickly. Most manuals include a **table of contents**, an **introduction**, and a series of specific sections that break down the technology being discussed. The **table of contents** helps users jump to the section they need, while the **introduction** often explains the manual's purpose and the intended audience—whether it's for beginners or more experienced users. For example, if you're dealing with a manual for a router, the table of contents might include sections on **installation**, **configuration**, **security settings**, and **troubleshooting**. Knowing where to find these sections can save you time and frustration.

In addition to structure, **precise language and terminology** play a huge role in understanding technical manuals. These documents often use industry-specific terms and acronyms that might be unfamiliar. Take, for instance, the term "**IP address**," which stands for **Internet Protocol address**. In networking manuals, this term is used frequently to explain how devices communicate over the internet. For IT professionals, understanding the exact meaning of such terms is crucial for implementing or troubleshooting systems effectively. Additionally, many manuals include **diagrams**, **screenshots**, and **flowcharts** to illustrate complex procedures. For example, a manual on server installation might include a flowchart showing the correct steps for setting up the server hardware and software, making it easier for a technician to follow.

Moreover, many technical manuals emphasize **safety guidelines** and **best practices**. Let's say you're working with an electrical component like a server power supply. The manual might include a safety warning, such as ensuring the device is grounded properly to avoid electrical shocks. Following these guidelines not only keeps you safe but also ensures compliance with industry standards. Often, manuals also have **troubleshooting sections** that walk users through common problems and solutions. For instance, if a router isn't connecting to the internet, a troubleshooting section might guide you through checking cables, restarting the device, and verifying network settings.

Staying **updated with technical manuals** is also key for career growth. As new technologies emerge, manufacturers regularly release new versions of manuals. Keeping up with these can help you stay current with the latest features and best practices. For example, a professional working with a cloud-based software tool should regularly review updates to the product's user guide to understand new features, functions, and integrations.

Analyzing Technical Articles and Research Papers

Reading and analyzing **technical articles** and **research papers** are vital skills for IT professionals who want to stay informed about the latest industry trends and innovations. These articles often present new methodologies, technologies, or case studies that could directly impact your work. For instance, a paper on **machine learning** might introduce a new algorithm that could make your data analysis tasks more efficient.

When approaching a **technical article**, it's helpful to understand its **structure**. A typical technical paper includes an **abstract**, **introduction**, **methodology**, **results**, and **discussion**. The **abstract** gives a brief overview of the entire paper, helping you decide if it's relevant to your work. For example, if you're reading an article on cloud security, the abstract will quickly tell you whether the paper covers a topic you need to know about. After reading the abstract, the next step is to dive into the **introduction** to understand the research question and its significance. If the paper is about new encryption techniques, the introduction will explain why this is an important topic in cybersecurity.

The **methodology** section explains how the research was conducted, including the tools and techniques used. For example, if a paper on cloud computing describes a new **load-balancing algorithm**, the methodology will outline how the researchers tested the algorithm in different environments, such as private vs. public cloud settings. This section is essential for understanding whether the findings are applicable to your own work. For instance, if the paper uses a methodology that doesn't match your environment, you might question the paper's relevance.

After understanding the methodology, you'll move to the **results** and **discussion** sections. These sections present the data and analyze the findings. If the article compares the effectiveness of two different cloud-based database solutions, the results will show which performed better. The **discussion** interprets the data and puts it in context. For example, the researchers might suggest that one solution is more scalable but costs more, while the other is cheaper but less reliable.

Finally, don't forget to explore the **references** and **citations**. These sources can lead you to more in-depth research on the topic.

Techniques for Improving Reading Speed and Comprehension

As an IT professional, you'll frequently encounter dense technical documents, such as **manuals**, **guides**, and

research papers. Developing skills to **read faster** and **retain more information** is crucial in this fast-paced environment. Here are some strategies:

1. **Skimming**: This technique involves quickly scanning the document to get the gist of it. For instance, if you're reading a manual for a new **project management tool**, you might skim the introduction to get a general sense of the tool's purpose, and then jump to the **troubleshooting** section if you're having a specific problem. Skimming helps you identify which sections need more attention, saving time while ensuring you don't miss important information.

2. **Chunking**: This method involves reading groups of words or phrases instead of individual words. For example, when reading code documentation, instead of reading each function line-by-line, try reading the code blocks as whole sections. This allows your brain to process larger chunks of information at once, speeding up reading and improving comprehension. When working with a list of commands, grouping related commands together in your mind can help you understand the overall flow of operations more efficiently.

3. **Active Reading**: This means engaging with the material rather than just passively absorbing it. For example, when reading a new technical guide on **network protocols**, take notes on key points, highlight important sections, or jot down questions

that arise. This helps reinforce your understanding and provides a reference for later.

4. **Limiting Subvocalization**: Many people naturally "say" the words in their head as they read, which can slow them down. Try to reduce this habit by focusing more on understanding the meaning behind the words rather than pronouncing them in your mind. For example, when reading about **API documentation**, try to focus on the structure and purpose of the code snippets rather than reading each word aloud in your head.

5. **Regular Practice**: The more you read, the better you'll get at it. By regularly reading **white papers**, **technical blogs**, and **manuals**, you'll get used to the language and structure of technical texts. Over time, this will improve both your speed and comprehension, helping you process information faster and with more accuracy.

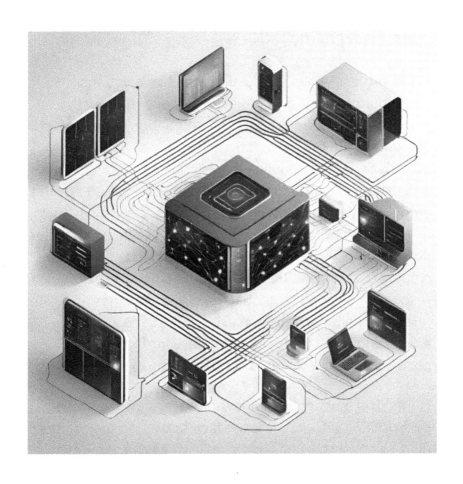

Chapter Five
Verbal Communication in IT

Conducting Effective Meetings

For IT professionals, conducting effective meetings is paramount to achieving project goals and maintaining smooth team collaboration. The foundation of a successful meeting lies in the preparation and clear definition of objectives. Before convening, it is critical to set clear goals and establish a structured agenda. A well-crafted agenda helps in setting expectations and ensures that all necessary topics are covered within a specific timeframe. For example, when discussing the deployment of a new cloud infrastructure, the agenda could include sections on resource allocation, potential risks, and timelines for testing and implementation. Distributing the agenda in advance allows attendees to prepare for the meeting, ensuring they are ready to contribute meaningfully.

During the meeting, maintaining focus and encouraging participation are vital. It is the facilitator's job to keep the discussion on track, making sure it stays aligned with the agenda. If the conversation veers off course, the facilitator must politely redirect it, ensuring that time is spent on critical issues. For instance, during a meeting about a software deployment, if the team starts discussing unrelated issues like office space management, the facilitator might gently steer them back to the topic of project deadlines. Ensuring that everyone has a chance to contribute is also key to a productive meeting. This can be achieved through techniques like round-robin, where each team member shares their input in turn, ensuring that no one is overlooked.

Additionally, documentation is crucial in meetings, particularly in the IT industry, where detailed technical discussions take place. Assigning a designated note-taker is essential for capturing important points, decisions, and action items. For instance, if the team decides on a new server configuration, the note-taker should clearly document the agreed-upon settings and who is responsible for testing them. Distributing these minutes shortly after the meeting reinforces accountability and ensures that participants are aligned on the next steps.

The use of technology can further enhance the effectiveness of meetings. Video conferencing tools, collaborative platforms like Google Docs or Microsoft Teams, and project management tools such as Jira can be leveraged to facilitate communication, especially when working with remote teams. IT professionals should be proficient in using these tools to streamline the meeting process, whether it's by sharing real-time documents, presenting data through screen sharing, or tracking action items directly in project management systems.

Finally, evaluating the effectiveness of meetings is crucial for continuous improvement. Gathering feedback from participants can help identify what worked well and what can be improved for future meetings. For example, if the team agrees that the meetings are often running overtime, feedback may reveal a need for a stricter time management approach. This reflective practice ensures that meetings remain a valuable and productive tool for collaboration.

Presenting Technical Information

Effectively presenting technical information is a crucial skill for IT professionals, as it enables them to communicate complex concepts to different audiences—whether to colleagues, clients, or non-technical stakeholders. The success of a presentation often hinges on the ability to tailor the content to the audience's knowledge level. For instance, when presenting a new data encryption protocol to senior management, an IT professional might focus on the business benefits—such as protecting customer data and ensuring compliance with regulatory standards—without delving into overly complex technical details. Conversely, when discussing the same topic with developers, the presentation could delve deeper into the underlying algorithms and implementation challenges.

The medium chosen for presenting the information also plays a significant role in the effectiveness of communication. Different tools—such as slideshows, whiteboards, or live demos—offer varying levels of engagement. For example, a slide deck might be useful for presenting an overview of a network architecture to a large audience, while a live demonstration of a new application might be more effective when showcasing its functionality to a small group of users. Visual aids, like graphs, charts, or diagrams, can be particularly helpful when presenting data-heavy topics, such as performance metrics or system uptime reports. These visuals help to break down complex data, making it more digestible and engaging for the audience.

Clarity and conciseness are essential when presenting technical information. It is crucial to avoid jargon or, if necessary, to explain it in layman's terms. For example, when explaining the concept of a RESTful API to a non-technical audience, an IT professional might compare it to a restaurant menu—where the customer (client) requests food (data) from the kitchen (server) by choosing from a menu (API). Analogies like this help to make the concept more relatable and accessible. Additionally, structuring the presentation in a logical flow—starting with the most basic concepts and progressively moving to more advanced topics—can prevent the audience from becoming overwhelmed.

Feedback is vital in any presentation. IT professionals should actively solicit questions and feedback during or after the presentation to gauge the audience's understanding. This allows them to clarify any points of confusion and adjust their approach if needed. For example, if a client expresses difficulty understanding the scalability of a database system, the presenter could offer further clarification by breaking down the scaling process into simpler terms or showing a real-world case study.

Lastly, refining presentation skills is an ongoing process that benefits from practice and experience. IT professionals should take every opportunity to present, whether in internal team meetings, client presentations, or industry conferences. Observing colleagues who excel in communication can provide valuable insights into improving one's presentation style. Over time, these practices help to build the confidence and proficiency required to present technical information effectively.

Engaging in Technical Discussions

Engaging in technical discussions is an essential skill for IT professionals, as it facilitates collaboration, knowledge sharing, and problem-solving. Given the complexity of IT concepts and the technical jargon often involved, the ability to communicate clearly and actively listen is paramount. Engaging in these discussions requires a balance of expressing one's own ideas and absorbing the perspectives of others. For instance, when discussing a new software architecture design with a development team, it is important to clearly explain the rationale behind specific design decisions, but also to remain open to feedback and suggestions that could improve the design.

Precision in language is critical during technical discussions. IT professionals must be adept at using terminology specific to their field, while also being mindful of the audience's familiarity with such terms. For example, when discussing a network security protocol with a client, an IT professional might avoid using terms like "BGP" (Border Gateway Protocol) unless the client is familiar with networking concepts. Instead, they could explain that BGP helps to determine the most efficient route for data to travel across the internet. Clarity in communication ensures that everyone involved in the discussion understands the issues at hand and can contribute meaningfully.

Active listening is another key element of successful technical discussions. IT professionals should engage with the speaker by summarizing key points and asking follow-up questions to ensure understanding. For example, if a team member is explaining a bug in a software system, an IT professional might say, "So, if I understand correctly, the issue occurs when the database connection times out, causing the app to crash. Is that right?" This not only shows that they are actively listening but also provides an opportunity for clarification.

Encouraging diverse perspectives is crucial in any technical discussion. IT professionals should foster an inclusive environment by encouraging quieter team members to share their thoughts or by using techniques such as round-robin sharing. For instance, in a meeting about choosing a cloud service provider, everyone—from system architects to security specialists—should have an opportunity to voice their opinions. This collaborative approach leads to more well-rounded discussions and can uncover insights that might otherwise be missed.

Finally, following up after technical discussions is essential for maintaining accountability and driving progress. Summarizing key takeaways and action items ensures that everyone is on the same page. This can be done through email, shared documents, or project management tools like Trello or Jira. For example, after discussing a new software feature, the meeting facilitator might send out a follow-up email outlining who is responsible for each task, along with deadlines and expectations. This helps ensure that decisions made during the discussion are acted upon and tracked, leading to more efficient project execution.

By engaging in technical discussions with clarity, active listening, and inclusivity, IT professionals can drive innovation and collaboration, ultimately leading to more successful project outcomes.

Chapter Six
Technical English in
Different IT Domains

Software Development

Software development is a systematic process that transforms an idea into a working application. This process typically follows several key stages: planning, design, coding, testing, and maintenance. Understanding each phase of the software development lifecycle (SDLC) is critical for IT professionals to ensure they meet client requirements, maintain quality, and handle challenges efficiently. Clear and precise communication at every stage is vital for collaboration among team members, clients, and stakeholders.

Planning Phase: The planning phase is the starting point for any software development project. During this stage, the requirements are gathered, and IT professionals collaborate closely with clients and stakeholders to understand their expectations. The clarity of communication during this phase is crucial, as it directly influences the direction of the project. For example, a project manager might conduct a requirements-gathering session, asking targeted questions to ensure that both technical and non-technical stakeholders have a clear understanding of the project's goals and limitations.

Design Phase: Once the requirements are defined, the design phase begins. IT professionals create a blueprint of the software's architecture, detailing its functionality and user interactions. This stage often involves wireframes, flowcharts, and user interface (UI) designs to communicate the structure of the software. For instance, a UI designer may present a wireframe for a new app, outlining how each screen will look and function, and engage in discussions with developers to ensure that the design aligns with technical feasibility.

Coding Phase: During the coding phase, the software is actually built. This is where programming skills come into play, and effective communication remains key. For example, developers often work in teams using version control systems like Git to track and merge changes. Here, frequent communication through commit messages, code reviews, and troubleshooting discussions ensures that the team remains aligned. A typical example of communication might be a developer explaining the reasoning behind a particular approach to solving a bug, or a pair of developers collaborating on a piece of code using pair programming techniques.

Testing Phase: The testing phase ensures that the software meets the requirements defined during the planning phase and functions as expected. Clear communication is needed to report bugs and suggest fixes. IT professionals must work with QA testers to identify and resolve issues quickly. For example, a tester might document a bug with detailed steps to reproduce it, allowing the developer to address the issue efficiently. Effective communication is key to ensuring that issues are resolved swiftly and that the software meets both functional and non-functional requirements.

Maintenance Phase: Maintenance follows the release of the software and is ongoing throughout its lifecycle. IT professionals must continue to communicate with users and other stakeholders to identify new issues or opportunities for improvement. For example, after a software release, developers may engage with users to receive feedback on usability, identifying areas where the software can be enhanced. This phase requires continuous collaboration and problem-solving to ensure the software continues to function properly over time.

Network Administration

Network administration is a foundational part of IT, focusing on the design, management, and optimization of network infrastructures. IT professionals in network administration must ensure that both hardware and software components function seamlessly to support business operations.

Network Infrastructure: Network administrators are responsible for setting up and maintaining network infrastructure, such as routers, switches, firewalls, and wireless access points. Clear communication with other departments and stakeholders is crucial when configuring these components to ensure optimal network performance. For instance, a network administrator may work with the security team to configure firewalls that protect sensitive company data. Effective communication ensures that the firewall rules are set up correctly without affecting necessary network traffic.

Monitoring Network Performance: Monitoring tools help network administrators assess the performance of the network and identify any issues before they escalate into critical problems. Administrators often use software to track data flow and bandwidth usage. For example, a network administrator might monitor the usage of a particular server and notice that it's nearing capacity, leading to the decision to upgrade its capabilities. This requires a combination of analytical skills and the ability to communicate the situation to management to justify the upgrade.

Security Measures: Security is one of the most critical aspects of network administration. Network administrators must implement security measures like firewalls, encryption, and intrusion detection systems to protect data. For example, after identifying a potential vulnerability, an administrator might work with the security team to patch the system and prevent a breach. Effective communication is essential here, as administrators need to clearly explain security threats and their mitigation strategies to both technical and non-technical stakeholders.

Collaboration and Communication: Network administrators often collaborate with other IT departments, such as support teams, developers, and security experts, to align network solutions with organizational goals. For instance, when implementing a new cloud-based service, the network administrator may need to collaborate with the cloud infrastructure team to ensure that the network can handle increased traffic without compromising performance. Effective communication is key in ensuring smooth operations and maintaining a stable network environment.

Cybersecurity

Cybersecurity is a rapidly growing field within IT, as threats to digital systems become increasingly sophisticated. IT professionals in cybersecurity must understand and manage risks to protect an organization's data, systems, and networks from cyberattacks.

Understanding Cyber Threats: Cybersecurity professionals must recognize various types of threats, including malware, phishing, ransomware, and denial-of-service attacks. Clear communication is essential when discussing the potential risks posed by these threats. For example, a cybersecurity expert might work with a company's leadership team to explain the risk of phishing attacks and implement a security awareness program. Additionally, cybersecurity professionals need to continuously monitor for emerging threats and adapt security strategies to counteract them.

Risk Management: One key aspect of cybersecurity is risk management, which involves identifying, evaluating, and mitigating potential risks. IT professionals must regularly assess vulnerabilities in systems and determine how to address them. For instance, when a new vulnerability is discovered in a widely used software, a cybersecurity expert might inform the organization's IT staff about the potential threat and advise on patching the system. Effective communication ensures that all teams are informed and can take appropriate action to minimize the risk.

Compliance and Regulatory Standards: Compliance with legal and regulatory requirements is another essential aspect of cybersecurity. Professionals must be familiar with regulations such as the General Data Protection Regulation (GDPR), the Health Insurance Portability and Accountability Act (HIPAA), and other data privacy laws. For example, a cybersecurity team might work with legal advisors to ensure that customer data is handled in compliance with GDPR. Communication with non-technical stakeholders is crucial to ensure that everyone in the organization understands the importance of data privacy and security.

Security Tools and Technologies: Cybersecurity professionals use various tools and technologies to secure systems and prevent cyberattacks. These include firewalls, intrusion detection systems, and encryption tools. IT professionals need to effectively communicate their technical knowledge of these tools to others within the organization. For instance, a cybersecurity expert may provide training for non-technical staff to recognize phishing emails and protect sensitive data.

Fostering a Cybersecurity Culture: In addition to implementing technical measures, cybersecurity professionals must foster a culture of security within the organization. This involves training employees on security best practices and raising awareness about potential threats. For example, a cybersecurity team might host regular workshops to educate employees on how to identify phishing attempts or maintain strong passwords. This proactive approach to cybersecurity helps reduce the risk of security breaches and empowers employees to protect themselves and the organization.

By understanding the unique communication needs in each IT domain, professionals can enhance their technical expertise and contribute more effectively to the success of their projects and organizations. Whether in software development, network administration, or cybersecurity, mastering the technical language of the field and being able to communicate complex concepts clearly are essential skills that drive both personal and organizational success.

Chapter Seven
Common Mistakes in Technical
English

Misuse of Technical Terms

The misuse of technical terms is one of the most frequent challenges faced in the IT industry. As technology evolves rapidly, the terminology associated with it can sometimes become confusing or misleading. The incorrect application of terms often results from a lack of understanding or an over-reliance on jargon. Miscommunication can arise, especially when technical language is misunderstood by both professionals and non-technical stakeholders, which can lead to project delays, incorrect implementations, or even financial losses.

A common mistake is the interchangeable use of terms like "software" and "hardware." While software refers to the programs or applications that run on a computer, hardware refers to the physical devices, such as the computer's CPU, memory, and input/output devices. If these terms are confused, a professional might suggest a software solution to resolve a hardware issue, causing inefficiencies and potentially leading to costly mistakes. Clear understanding and proper usage of these terms are essential for effective collaboration, especially when explaining technical concepts to clients or non-technical team members.

Another area of frequent miscommunication occurs within cybersecurity discussions. For instance, terms such as "virus," "malware," and "ransomware" are often used interchangeably, even though they represent different types of threats. A virus refers to a type of malware that can replicate itself and spread to other systems, whereas ransomware locks files and demands payment for their release. Misusing these terms could lead to confusion and may result in the wrong type of protective measures being applied. It's vital that IT professionals are clear on the differences between such terms to ensure they address the right security risks effectively.

The global nature of the IT industry can also introduce challenges. Professionals from different linguistic backgrounds may encounter difficulties in translating technical terms accurately. Some terms may not have direct equivalents in other languages, leading to misinterpretations. Establishing a common glossary or set of definitions within multicultural teams is a practical approach to mitigate these issues. By ensuring that everyone is aligned on what each term means, the likelihood of misunderstanding decreases significantly.

To avoid the misuse of technical terms, IT professionals should engage in continuous learning to keep up with evolving terminologies. Participating in training, attending industry workshops, or enrolling in technical writing courses can greatly enhance one's understanding of terminology. Additionally, promoting a culture where team members feel comfortable seeking clarification and asking questions ensures that everyone remains on the same page.

Grammatical Errors in Technical Writing

Grammatical mistakes in technical writing can diminish the clarity and professionalism of documents. In the IT field, where precision is crucial, grammatical errors can result in misinterpretations of instructions, system configurations, or technical specifications, potentially leading to errors in project execution.

One of the most common mistakes is the misuse of subject-verb agreement. This error occurs when the subject and verb in a sentence do not match in number. For instance, "The system were tested" should be corrected to "The system was tested." Such mistakes might seem minor but can create confusion, especially when working on technical specifications or instructions where accuracy is paramount. IT professionals should develop the habit of reviewing sentences to ensure that they are grammatically correct, particularly when dealing with technical documents that will be used by others.

In addition, inconsistent tense usage is another frequent grammatical issue. Technical writing often requires using specific tenses to describe ongoing processes, completed tasks, or future actions. For instance, in documenting a system upgrade, IT professionals may need to describe what has been done (past tense), what is happening (present tense), and what will be done (future tense). Mixing these tenses in the same document can confuse readers and obscure the timeline of events

Sentence fragments also pose a challenge in technical writing. A sentence fragment occurs when a group of words does not form a complete thought. For example, "When the system is updated." This phrase leaves the reader expecting more information and lacks a subject or an independent clause. In technical writing, each sentence must convey a complete idea, especially when describing procedures or system requirements. Clear, complete sentences ensure that readers can follow the instructions or technical specifications without confusion.

To address these issues, IT professionals should invest time in refining their grammar skills. Regularly reviewing and editing technical documents, using grammar check tools, and seeking feedback from colleagues can help identify and correct errors. A commitment to grammatical accuracy will not only enhance the quality of technical documents but also boost the writer's credibility and professionalism.

Avoiding Ambiguity in Communication

Ambiguity in communication can lead to significant problems in IT projects. When messages are unclear or open to interpretation, the risk of misunderstandings and mistakes increases, potentially delaying projects and causing confusion. IT professionals must prioritize clarity and precision in their communication to avoid costly errors and ensure that their messages are easily understood.

One effective way to avoid ambiguity is through the use of specific terminology. In IT, many terms have very precise meanings that must be conveyed accurately. Instead of using vague or general words like "some" or "many," it's better to be specific. For instance, instead of saying, "There is some increase in system performance," an IT professional should say, "The system performance has increased by 20%." Specificity in language ensures that the message is clear and actionable, leaving little room for misinterpretation.

Another useful strategy is to structure communication logically. Well-organized messages are easier to follow and understand. When presenting complex information, IT professionals can use outlines, bullet points, or numbered lists to break down the content into smaller, digestible parts. This structure helps the reader follow the sequence of ideas and ensures that key points stand out. Additionally, using headings and subheadings can provide a clear roadmap, guiding the reader through the document and enhancing overall comprehension.

In addition to logical structure, seeking feedback from colleagues and peers is a valuable way to ensure clarity. Engaging others in the review process can help identify areas where the message might still be unclear. Encouraging questions during discussions and offering explanations when needed can further reduce ambiguity. Feedback loops are essential for refining communication and ensuring that it is understood as intended.

Visual aids, such as diagrams, flowcharts, and graphs, are another powerful tool for eliminating ambiguity. Complex technical concepts can often be better explained through visual representations. For example, a network diagram can show how different systems are interconnected, providing a clearer understanding than a text-based explanation alone. Visual aids can also serve as a reference point for future discussions, reinforcing the message and aiding retention.

By employing these strategies—using specific language, structuring communication logically, seeking feedback, and using visual aids—IT professionals can significantly reduce ambiguity and improve the effectiveness of their communication. Clear communication not only enhances collaboration within teams but also ensures that technical knowledge is accurately conveyed to clients, stakeholders, and non-technical audiences.

Chapter Eight
Enhancing Technical English Skills

Resources for Continuous Improvement

Continuous improvement is crucial for IT professionals to stay competitive and advance in their careers. The fast-paced nature of the IT industry demands constant learning, and numerous resources are available to help professionals enhance their technical English skills. These resources cater specifically to the needs of IT professionals and range from online courses and certifications to books, professional organizations, and peer collaboration. By taking advantage of these tools, IT professionals can strengthen both their technical and communication abilities, which are essential for success in today's globalized and rapidly changing tech environment.

Online Platforms for Training and Skill Enhancement

Online learning platforms are an excellent resource for IT professionals seeking to improve their technical English skills and stay up-to-date with industry trends. Websites such as Coursera, Udemy, and LinkedIn Learning offer flexible courses in technical writing, programming languages, communication in IT environments, and more. These platforms often feature courses taught by industry experts and allow learners to complete lessons at their own pace. By engaging with these resources, professionals not only improve their technical English but also keep themselves informed about the latest developments in IT technologies.

Moreover, many online platforms offer specialized courses for certification preparation. Certification is a valuable tool in validating expertise in a specific IT domain, such as cybersecurity, software development, or networking. By earning certifications, IT professionals gain credibility and increase their employability. Many online courses are designed with certification exams in mind, ensuring that professionals not only learn the necessary concepts but also develop the communication skills required to explain complex topics in a concise, clear manner.

Books and Publications for Technical English Mastery

Books focused on technical English offer in-depth guidance on writing documentation, drafting technical reports, and communicating in a professional IT environment. Titles dedicated to effective communication in technical fields often cover topics such as structuring technical documents, understanding the nuances of technical jargon, and improving clarity in written communication. Reading books that focus on technical writing can also help professionals familiarize themselves with the tone and style expected in the IT industry.

Subscribing to professional journals, magazines, and newsletters also helps professionals stay current with industry trends and new developments in the field. These resources frequently discuss new technologies and best practices for communication in IT, offering valuable insights into the evolving needs of IT professionals. By keeping up with publications, professionals can also stay informed about ongoing research and developments, ensuring that their technical language remains relevant and accurate.

Professional Organizations for Networking and Learning

Professional organizations such as the Association for Computing Machinery (ACM), the Institute of Electrical and Electronics Engineers (IEEE), and other tech-focused groups provide networking opportunities, resources, and events aimed at fostering professional growth. These organizations often host workshops, webinars, and conferences that cover technical communication skills and provide a platform for members to discuss industry-specific challenges. Joining such associations helps IT professionals expand their networks, share knowledge with peers, and access exclusive resources that promote continuous learning.

Peer Feedback and Collaborative Projects

Peer feedback and collaborative projects are highly effective for continuous improvement in both technical skills and language proficiency. Working on team-based projects allows IT professionals to practice technical English in a real-world context. Participating in code reviews, documentation writing, and project discussions gives professionals the opportunity to refine their communication skills by receiving constructive feedback from colleagues. Engaging in collaborative efforts promotes knowledge sharing and fosters an environment of collective learning, which is essential for professional growth.

Creating study groups, online forums, or discussion platforms within teams can also help professionals develop their technical English proficiency. Through collaborative discussions, team members can share insights, clarify technical concepts, and reinforce learning. This type of peer interaction fosters a learning culture, where IT professionals can enhance both their technical and language skills, resulting in more effective communication and improved project outcomes.

Online Courses and Certifications

Online courses and certifications have revolutionized how IT professionals develop new skills and enhance their knowledge base. The rapid evolution of technology means that staying updated is crucial, and online platforms provide a flexible and convenient way to achieve this goal. Many online courses are designed to allow learners to work at their own pace, making it possible for IT professionals to learn while balancing their professional responsibilities.

Wide Range of Available Courses

Online platforms offer courses on a wide range of topics relevant to IT professionals. From mastering programming languages and software development methodologies to understanding the complexities of cybersecurity and data analysis, there is a course for almost every area of IT. Many courses include multimedia elements like video lectures, interactive exercises, and hands-on projects, which cater to different learning preferences and ensure a comprehensive learning experience. The variety of courses available also enables professionals to specialize in a particular area or broaden their knowledge to encompass a wide range of skills.

Importance of Certifications

Certifications play a pivotal role in validating an IT professional's expertise in a particular field. Popular certifications, such as CompTIA, Cisco, Microsoft, and AWS, are widely recognized in the industry and demonstrate a professional's ability to apply their technical knowledge in real-world scenarios. Certification programs often include exams that test both technical and language proficiency, reinforcing the importance of mastering clear and effective communication when working with complex systems and technologies.

In addition to validating skills, certifications enhance the professional's résumé and increase their chances of being considered for high-demand roles. Earning certifications through online courses demonstrates a commitment to continuous learning and professional development, which is highly valued by employers. As new technologies emerge, having up-to-date certifications can help professionals remain competitive and position themselves as experts in their respective fields.

Networking Opportunities

Online learning platforms also facilitate networking opportunities that can enhance professional growth. Many platforms offer forums, discussion groups, and virtual events where learners can interact with instructors and peers. These interactions help professionals expand their network, share knowledge, and seek advice from others in the industry. Online communities can also provide insights into job opportunities and trends in the industry, making them valuable resources for career advancement.

Networking and Professional Development Opportunities

Networking and professional development are integral aspects of an IT professional's career. Building relationships with other professionals, mentors, and industry leaders opens doors to new opportunities and helps individuals stay informed about emerging technologies and trends. Active participation in networking events, both online and in person, fosters collaboration and a sense of community within the industry.

The Role of Networking in Professional Growth

Networking helps IT professionals stay connected with industry experts and peers, which can lead to new job opportunities, collaborations, and valuable advice. Conferences, online forums, and local meetups are excellent venues for networking, as they allow individuals to learn from others, exchange ideas, and build relationships that may prove valuable over the long term. In addition, connecting with mentors can help professionals navigate career challenges and gain insights into navigating the complex IT landscape.

Workshops, Webinars, and Certification Programs

In addition to networking, IT professionals should invest in workshops, webinars, and certification programs that focus on professional development. These events are excellent opportunities to gain new knowledge, enhance skills, and engage with industry leaders. Participating in these events can help professionals stay current with advancements in technology and refine their communication skills for a technical environment. Many professional organizations and online platforms host such events, offering an accessible and affordable means of continuing education.

Building Relationships through Online Platforms

Platforms such as LinkedIn, GitHub, and specialized online communities are essential tools for IT professionals looking to expand their professional networks. These platforms enable individuals to share their work, discuss projects, and connect with others in the industry. Additionally, they offer a way for professionals to stay informed about job openings, industry trends, and professional development opportunities, making them invaluable for career advancement.

Mentorship and Peer Support

Mentorship is another important aspect of networking and professional development. Establishing a mentor-mentee relationship provides IT professionals with personalized guidance and support throughout their careers. Mentors can offer advice based on their experiences and help mentees set and achieve career goals. Conversely, IT professionals can also benefit from mentoring others, which allows them to reinforce their knowledge, develop leadership skills, and contribute to the growth of the profession.

Networking and mentorship create an environment conducive to learning, growth, and career advancement, helping IT professionals stay competitive in an ever-evolving industry.

Resource Bank

Here is a comprehensive list of resources for future learning to help IT professionals improve both their technical and English communication skills:

Online Learning Platforms

1. **Coursera**
   Offers courses from top universities and organizations on topics like programming, cybersecurity, data science, and communication skills in IT. Many courses also offer certification.
   www.coursera.org

2. **IEEE Learning Network**
   Offers extensive online learnings for Technical Professionals in all IT,& most Engineering Fields
   https://lln.ieee.org

3. **Udemy**
   A large platform with a wide variety of IT courses, including technical English, software development, and network security. Courses are taught by industry experts and often include lifetime access.
   www.udemy.com

4. **LinkedIn Learning**
   Provides professional development courses in various IT topics, including communication skills, coding, and software management. Often offers free trials.
   www.linkedin.com/learning

5. **Pluralsight**
   Known for in-depth tech-focused courses, it offers paths
   and certifications in areas like cloud computing,
   programming, data analytics, and soft skills.
   www.pluralsight.com

6. **edX**
   Offers free and paid courses from universities and
   institutions on technical topics such as computer science,
   cybersecurity, and artificial intelligence.
   www.edx.org

7. **FutureLearn**
   Provides online courses on a variety of IT and technical
   communication topics, including cybersecurity, coding,
   and digital communication skills.
   www.futurelearn.com

Books for Technical English and Communication Skills

1. **"The Elements of Style" by William Strunk Jr. and E.B. White**
   A timeless resource for improving clarity and precision in writing.

2. **"Technical Communication" by Mike Markel**
   A textbook focused on technical writing skills, such as writing reports, user guides, and instructions in an easy-to-understand manner.

3. **"Writing for Computer Science" by Justin Zobel**
   Offers guidance on writing clear, concise technical documents, specifically aimed at those in the computer science field.

4. **"The Chicago Manual of Style"**
   A comprehensive reference book for writing and formatting technical documents, especially useful for technical writers in IT.

5. **"Business Writing for Results" by R. L. Krach and M. J. R. Wright**
   Helps IT professionals improve their written communication for business and technical audiences.

6. **"The Art of Technical Documentation" by Ben Salama**
   A practical guide to technical writing that covers aspects such as structure, language, and visuals in technical documents.

Certifications and Specialized Learning Resources

1. **CompTIA Certifications (e.g., CompTIA IT Fundamentals, CompTIA A+, CompTIA Security+)**
   A widely recognized suite of certifications in IT fundamentals, networking, and security.
   www.comptia.org

2. **Cisco Certifications (e.g., CCNA, CCNP)**
   Offers foundational to advanced certifications in networking, widely respected in the IT industry.
   www.cisco.com

3. **Microsoft Certifications (e.g., Microsoft Certified: Azure Fundamentals, Windows Server)**
   Provides certifications for cloud computing, networking, and server management.
   learn.microsoft.com

4. **AWS Certification (Amazon Web Services)**
   A leading cloud computing platform that offers certifications in areas like cloud architecture, development, and operations.
   aws.amazon.com/certification

5. **Google Professional Certifications**
   Google offers professional certifications for roles in IT support, data analytics, and cloud computing.
   https://cloud.google.com/training

6.

7. **Certified Information Systems Security Professional (CISSP)**
   A certification for IT professionals working in cybersecurity and network security.
   www.isc2.org

8. **Scrum Certification (e.g., Certified ScrumMaster, Certified Scrum Product Owner)**
   For IT professionals working in Agile environments, Scrum certifications focus on project management and team collaboration.
   www.scrumalliance.org

Professional Organizations and Communities

1. **IEEE (Institute of Electrical and Electronics Engineers)**
   Offers conferences, publications, and networking opportunities for professionals in electronics, engineering, and IT.
   www.ieee.org

2. **ACM (Association for Computing Machinery)**
   A professional organization offering resources, conferences, and journals dedicated to computing and information technology.
   www.acm.org

3. **ISACA (Information Systems Audit and Control Association)**
   Specializes in IT governance, risk management, and cybersecurity with certifications such as CISA and CISM.
   www.isaca.org

4. **ITProTV**
   Provides training, resources, and certifications for IT professionals in a variety of fields, including cloud computing, security, and network management.
   www.itpro.tv

5. **TechWellness**
   A platform focused on improving digital wellness and skills, including online courses for IT professionals looking to improve communication in a tech environment.
   www.techwellness.com

6. **GitHub**
   A platform where developers collaborate on code, open-source projects, and share knowledge. It's also a great place for IT professionals to improve communication and collaboration skills.
   www.github.com

7. **Stack Overflow**
   A community-driven Q&A platform for developers where IT professionals can ask technical questions, engage in discussions, and share insights.
   www.stackoverflow.com

Discussion Forums and Communities

1. **Reddit: r/learnprogramming**
   A community for learning programming and technology skills, where users can ask questions and share resources.
   www.reddit.com/r/learnprogramming

2. **Stack Exchange (IT, Programming, and Tech Sites)**
   A network of Q&A websites dedicated to various fields in IT, including software development, IT support, and cybersecurity.
   www.stackexchange.com

3. **Dev.to**
   A platform for developers to share ideas, discuss coding issues, and publish articles on the latest trends in technology and software development.
   www.dev.to

Additional Resources for Practicing Technical English

1. **Grammarly**
   An online tool that helps correct grammar, spelling, punctuation, and sentence structure. It's useful for improving both technical and general writing.
   www.grammarly.com

2. **Hemingway Editor**
   A tool that helps simplify and clarify writing by highlighting complex sentences and grammar mistakes, ideal for enhancing technical writing.
   www.hemingwayapp.com

3. **Write the Docs**
   A community dedicated to documentation and technical writing, offering resources such as guides, conferences, and articles.
   www.writethedocs.org

4. **Google Scholar**
   For IT professionals looking for research papers and academic articles, Google Scholar provides access to a wide array of scholarly literature on technical topics.
   scholar.google.com

Dedication

To every IT professional who has ever navigated the labyrinth of technical jargon, debugged a late-night issue, or translated the language of code into something humanly understandable—this book is for you.

May it empower you to break language barriers, communicate with confidence, and inspire the next generation of innovators.

Thank you for building the systems that move the world forward.

— With immense gratitude

الحمد لله